A selection of words and anecdotes
from around Leicestershire

by
Diane Davies

BRADWELL
BOOKS

Published by Bradwell Books
9 Orgreave Close Sheffield S13 9NP
Email: books@bradwellbooks.co.uk

British Library Cataloguing in Publication Data: a catalogue record for this book is available from the British Library.

1st Edition

ISBN: 9781910551103

Typesetting by: Andrew Caffrey

Photograph Credits: Leicestershire County Council & iStock

Print: Gomer Press, Llandysul, Ceredigion SA44 4JL

Introduction

Although not from Leicestershire myself, I lived in the county for eleven years from 2001 to 2012 while working as a lecturer at the University of Leicester. My interest in the regional dialect began almost as soon as I had moved to the area and started to notice things about the accents and expressions of people born and bred in the locality. It wasn't long before I heard the word *mardy* and the address form *me duck* in Leicester market, and passing some window cleaners heard one of them refer to *uz ladders*. Some time later I started to use examples of recorded Leicestershire speech in my teaching of sociolinguistics, and this led to an opportunity to do some research on the East Midlands dialect and, more specifically, the Leicestershire variety. One project I undertook, called *Village Voices*, involved collaboration with some of the county's Heritage Wardens to record the speech of people of different generations who had spent all or most of their lives in the same Leicestershire villages.

We tend to take the variety of English we speak for granted most of the time, but when we meet people from other areas of the country we quickly notice the subtle differences between varieties or dialects. A female resident of Thringstone interviewed for the *Village Voices* study said:

I am really not aware of my accent, but when you visit other districts/areas, other people know I am from Leicestershire.

Another interviewee from the same village, aged 75, came to the even more precise conclusion: *I do think in a lot of respects I'm broad Thringstone.*

Those participating were asked to write down any local words or phrases they might use to express particular meanings on a list. For the meaning *'ask someone to wait'* a 38-year-old wrote *ode on ('hold on')*, his deliberately creative spelling reflecting how the *'l'* in that position is sometimes dropped in a Leicestershire accent. For the same reason he also wrote *cowd* to represent his way of pronouncing *'cold'*. This feature is often seen in written representations of the dialect of the East Midlands.

Some often-referred-to terms associated with different areas of the country (not restricted to a single county) include words for a path or alleyway between houses, for being left-handed, and for actions such as avoiding school (*mitching, bunking off, skiving,* etc.). These seem quite resilient across different generations, with both older and younger people saying they use the terms *jitty*, *caggy-handed* or *bunk off*, for example. However, it will come as no surprise, I'm sure, that words for many other things are subject to fashion and can differ markedly between generations. For the concept of 'attractive (person)', for instance, older respondents suggested they might say *stunning*, while the words used by younger people from the same villages included *fit* and *peng*.

The participants in our study said they were proud of their regional accent and of the villages they came from. Some bemoaned the erosion of the close-knit rural communities they remembered from their youth, but they also appreciated the way village halls and a range of local societies could still bring people together and build a sense of local identity. They felt the Leicestershire dialect was still alive and kicking, despite the fact that a sense of shared community was, in some places at least, less tangible than it used to be.

Looking back

The 'prestige' variety or dialect we call Standard English had its roots in the East Midlands dialect of Middle English. Today it is an international variety taught in our schools and across the world, the recognised norm in both writing and speech for educated users of English.

In the Middle English period it is generally agreed there were four main dialect areas: Northern (extending southwards to the Humber), East Midland, West Midland and Southern (south of the Thames together with Gloucestershire and parts of Hereford and Worcester). The East and West Midland dialects covered the area between the Humber and the Thames, but by this time they were distinct from each other because only the East Midland dialect area had previously been subject to Danish (Viking) rule within the territory of the Danelaw. This had of course brought many Scandinavian words into the English of the East Midland area, seen in place names and some everyday vocabulary, for example the many words with an '*sk*' sound, like *sky*, *bask*, *skirt* and *skill*. By the late 14th century, the East Midland dialect area was the most populous and had more valuable agricultural land than the north and west at the time, so wealthy merchants from this part of the country became influential in London, now the centre of power. As an intermediate dialect between northern and southern, it was also more comprehensible to all at a time when people from areas far apart had considerable difficulty in understanding each other.

Today accent is often the first clue we have to someone's regional background. We might guess whether they come from the 'north' or the 'south' of England, for instance, by the way they pronounce words like *laugh*, *class* or *pub*. But what about the way they say *make*, *school*, *town* or *few*? And how do they say *isn't?* Sometimes the most helpful clues to regional dialect are found in the less obvious features.

One thing worth remembering is that, even though it is possible to talk about 'Leicestershire dialect', it is at the same time the East Midlands dialect, having much in common with that of Nottinghamshire, Derbyshire and Lincolnshire (allowing for some differences between them, of course!). Regional dialects do not simply follow county boundaries on the map. Their range is shaped more by historical borders such as the main travel routes, rivers and hill ranges or by the location of important centres for trade. Where there has been much commerce between two neighbouring regions, their dialects can shade into each other, but where contact has been infrequent we find more marked differences between the two dialects. County boundaries are, in any case, unreliable in another way: their exact position is sometimes changed at the whim of governments. Leicestershire and Rutland exemplify this quite well.

Today we might assume that regional dialects are dying out because we move around the country (and world) much more than in the past, we're connected through 24-hour media wherever we live, and because the traditional rural way of life is fast disappearing. Certainly, some of the older dialect words and expressions collected for this book are no longer in use. Nevertheless, there are still words, expressions and accents that are instantly associated with different regions. Just as a living language is always in a state of flux, so its regional dialects change too, abandoning certain words, using others in new ways, and absorbing new elements with every generation.

I hope this little book will make you more aware of and interested in Leicestershire dialect, past and present, whether you are from the county, a new resident, or a visitor. The dialect dictionary has terms from a range of sources to give a flavour, mainly, of the traditional dialect. A few items are not, strictly, dialect words but are included simply to represent the local accent through non-standard spelling. I have avoided, though, the kind of condensed spelling sometimes found in lists of dialect phrases intended as puzzles or jokes about accent, such as *Supwiyo* for 'What's up with you?' – these can be pretty baffling if you're not an insider! The topics and anecdotes that follow the dictionary are an eclectic mix of information from a range of sources and include some transcribed extracts from speech recorded in more recent times in different parts of Leicestershire.

Glossary

A

Abear – endure or tolerate

Ackern – acorn

Adam's ale – cold water

Addle – earn wages (addlins: earnings, wages)

Adeal – much, greatly (a deal of – a lot of)

Adlands – headlands or unploughed part of field

Admire – be pleased or gratified

Afore – before

Agen – against, near, next to (*'A stood it agen the door'*)

Ahent – behind (also ahind, pronounced *'a-hoind'*)

Ahsomdivver – howsoever

Akedok – aqueduct

All-as-is – the sum total, the whole of the matter

Allus – always

A'most – almost

Anigh – near, close

Apern – apron

Argufy – argue or wrangle, or to signify something

Arm-hole – armpit

Arr aint yorn – that isn't yours

Arsy-versy – topsy-turvy, upside down

Asking – publication of the banns of marriage

A-that'n(s) – in that way or manner

At the minute – at the moment

Aught – anything

Aust – dare

Awkward – ill-tempered

Aye and like! – yes, certainly

Azzled – rough and chapped like hands in frosty weather; sour; churlish

B

Backen – hinder, repress

Back-end – autumn and early winter

Bad – difficult, hard

Baddish – rather bad

Badge – cut and tie up beans in shocks or sheaves

Badly – sickly, in bad health

Bailey – bailiff

Band – bond

Banger – anything huge or extraordinary, particularly a huge fib

Barnish – fill out, grow fat

Bash – dwindle, become sickly

Beast – beasts, especially horned cattle

Bettermost – superior

Big time – to a great extent

Black over Bill's mother's – it looks like rain
Blether – cry, blubber, also to be out of breath
Blort – chide in a loud tone
Brangle – wrangle, quarrel; branglement – confusion
Brock – a badger
Broom-dasher – maker or seller of brooms
Brummagem – counterfeit, sham (variant of 'Birmingham')
Buck-bearing – teasing, finding fault
Buffer – stupid fellow (blockhead)
Bungole – cheese
By times – sometimes

C

Caddling – dainty, fastidious
Cadge – beg, hawk small goods
Cank about – carry tales, gossip
Chanceable – precarious, liable to sudden change
Chary – economical, careful, solicitous
Chelp – chirp, chatter (like a magpie)
Chimble – chew, nibble or munch in a ruminating manner
Chuff – pleased, delighted
Clam – starve, famish (also clem)
Clank – set or series
Clarty – state of ground after hard frost
Clicking room – area where leather is cut out in shoe making

Clot – break up clods in a field after harrowing, also scatter manure left on grazing land
Coddie – foreman
Coggie – swimming costume
Contrive – imagine, comprehend
Cope – bid money for, bargain for
Cow-gate – the right to have a cow graze on lanes (a privilege once given to the poor at Wymeswold and other villages)
Coxy – touchy, conceited, supercilious
Crack – boast, brag
Cram – intrude
Crank, cranky – sick, ailing
Crawk – make a hoarse noise, caw, call out loudly
Croaker – doctor
Crump – mix, stir or fold in
Cut – canal

D

Dab – small amount
Dade – indeed
Daffadowndilly – daffodil
Dag – to trail in the dirt
Dapstuck – prim, dapper, proper
Dark-hour – the last evening twilight

Delft – a spade's depth

Demeanour – eccentricity

Denial – hindrance, trial

Dither – shiver, shudder

Do for – to clean, cook and wash for someone

Do with –put up with, tolerate

Docible – docile, teachable

Doddipole – a simpleton

Done in – tired

Dooish – active, handy

Dredgery – carefully, gently, 'gingerly'

Durst – to dare

E

Earable – arable

Easings – eaves (of a stack or rick)

Edgy – eager

Een't –am not, is not, are not, have not

Else – or else, otherwise (also elseways)

Elseways – otherwise

Embranglement – embroilment and confusion

Endlong – endways

Enew – enough (also enow)

E's gorra chin on – he's in a grumpy mood

Ever so – very much (*'Ah couldn't dew it, not if it wur ivver so'*

– i.e. no matter what pressure I were under)

Expect – infer, suppose

Eyeable – pleasing to the eye

Ey up – greeting (as in *'Ey up me duck!'*)

F

Faddle – to indulge, humour, pet

Faddy – fanciful, fastidious

Fairish – considerable in amount, size, number ('it's fairish warm')

Fantodds – indisposition (*'he's got the fantodds'*)

Farrantly – neat, trim, lively (was generally used as an epithet for a girl)

Fast-sure – perfectly sure, certain

Favour – resemble (*'she fevours 'er moother'*)

Feast – a 'wake' or annual fair held in villages, usually in the summer or autumn

Feelth – feeling, sensation

Fetch – bring

Fetchel – tease, provoke (*'I oon'y did it to fetchel 'im'*)

Fir-apple – a fir-cone

Fire-tail – the redstart

Firking – itching

Fleer – gibe, jest or sneer

Folks – people

For all – in spite of, notwithstanding

Friggle – be tediously particular over something

G

Ganzi – jumper

Gattards – towards the gate, i.e. 'gatewards'

Gen – gave (*'he gen him a tenner'*)

Get shut of – get rid of

Get the hump – be annoyed

Gie – give (*'gie it here'*)

Gis a gleg – let me have a look (give me a look)

Give over – stop

Gloppen – tendency to sickness or palpitations

Go off – go on, happen (*'What's gooin' off?'*)

Gorra bag on – in a mood

Groudly – grumbling, discontented

Gurgle – gullet

Gyp – ridicule, verbal abuse

H

Had ought – ought

Hagging – trying, fatiguing, aggravating

Ham-gams – antics, tricks (*'A's bin at some o' his hamgans agen.'*)

Hand-over-head – inconsiderately, indiscriminately,

without concern for the consequences

Hard-set – in difficulties, under pressure

Harry-long-legs – daddy-long-legs

Hasky – harsh, rough

Heart-alive! – exclamation of surprise

Hedge-jugg – the long-tailed tit

Hern – hers

Het up – riled, angry

Hisn – his

Hoigh and loike – assuredly (corruption of '*aye and like*')

Holts – debates or disputes

Hoomble-Coom-Booz – bumble bee

Hully – wholly

Hust, husting – cough, coughing (German – *husten*)

I

Iggle – icicle

Ill-convenient – inconvenient

Ill-willy – malevolent, malicious

Indifferent – middling, neither good nor bad

Inion – onion (*'Diff'rent people have diff'rent 'pinions, Some like apples an' some like inions.'*)

Ink-horn – an inkstand

Insense – inform, apprise

In't – isn't (Int it – isn't it)

I'steads – instead

Itter – cross, hostile, ill-natured (*'A wur very itter agen 'er.'*)

Ivvel – evil (*'when we got there, she looked at us as ivvel as ivvel.'*)

J

Jack-in-the-hedge – hedge-mustard, or hedge-garlic

Jack-squealer – the swift

Jack-towel – a kitchen towel hung on a roller

Jagg – large bundle of briars used for breaking the clods in a ploughed field

Jaunders – jaundice

Jib – refuse to move forwards (usually with reference to horses)

Jibble – jingle, rattle

Jiggin! – *'gee again'*, said to horses to get them to turn to the off side

Jingling – careless, slipshod (*'A goos abaout it in a jinglin' sort of way'*)

Jitty – common passageway between two houses

Jobbet – a small load or cart-load

Jolter-headed – stupid, foolish

Jowl – to strike, knock

Jumbal – thin, crisp cake with carraway seeds, S-shaped (associated with Market Bosworth)

Jup! – *'gee-up'*

Just-now-since – a very short time ago

Justly – exactly (*'Ah doon't joostly knoo'*)

K

Keck – to feel sick or squeamish (*'It meks me kek to think on't'*)

Khazi – toilet

Kibble – to 'bruise' or crush oats or other corn

Kick – to sting (e.g. wasp)

Kids – little faggots

Kimnel – large tub used for whey

Kit – clothes

Kitling – kitten

Kiver – cover (of a tub, e.g. butter-kiver)

Knibs – the two projections on the snead by which the mower handles the scythe

Knock-along – get on quickly

Know to – know of something

Knowledge – to get beyond one's knowledge was to get into a locality one didn't know, to lose one's way

L

Laggy bands – elastic bands

Laid – applied to grass, corn, etc. beaten down by the wind

Lamb-Hog – yearling sheep

Land – one of the main divisions in a ploughed field
Larrup – thrash, wallop
Lash / lash-horse – the second horse in a team
Last – trace left on the ground by the foot (also last-making in the footwear industry). Source of idiom 'stick/keep to one's last' (i.e. one's usual area of expertise)
Lather – ladder
Learn – teach
Leastways / leastwise – at least
Lief – rather, willing
Likely – promising (*'A loikely lad'*)
Lines – certificate of marriage (marriage-lines)
Looked on – respected by others
Look out – lengthen (e.g. days lengthening)
Lowk – to beat or thrash
Lungeous – violent, quarrelsome
Lushy – rather drunk (full of *'lush'* or strong drink)

M

Malkin – a scarecrow
Mang – confused mass or mixture (*'All of a mang loike'*)
M'appen – perhaps, possibly (*'may happen'*)
Mardy – grumpy, irritable, sulky
Marls – marbles
Mash – to make tea

Massacred – embarrassed
Maumy – soft, overcooked
Me duck – form of address
Mere – boundary (mere-thurrow: furrow marking a boundary)
Minted – rich
Mither – to puzzle, perplex, daze, confuse (*'moithered with heat'*)
Mizzle – to drizzle
Moffle – to mumble (*'muffle'*) one's words
Moire – mire (*'one's as deep i' the mud, as the tother i' the moire'*)
Mun – must

N

Nab – catch, capture
Nah – now
Natty – neat, trim, tasteful
Navigation – a canal
Nayther – neither (also *noyther*)
Nayzen – birds' nests (sometimes *neezen*)
Near-hand – almost, nearly, probably
Neighbouring – gossiping among the neighbours
Nesh – weak, susceptible to cold
Never-a-deal – not much
Nigh-agen – probably, most likely
Nivver – never

Noddy – sleepy
Nor – than (also *nur*)
Nowt – nought, nothing (sometimes pronounced '*note*')
Nunty – trim, dapper

O

Oakey – ice cream
Oast – to incline, lean, tend in a particular direction
O'er-by-yon – yonder
O'er-wart – opposite ('*over-thwart*')
Off-the-hooks – shabby, worn out, ailing
Offy – off licence
One-how(s) – somehow
One while – at one time
Opiniated – opinionated, obstinate
Orts – scraps, fragments
Ourn – ours
Out-asked – a betrothed couple were said to be out-asked when their banns of marriage had been published three times
Outside – extreme, excessive ('*he gave an outside price for the horse*')
Over-get – get over something (e.g. death of a loved one)
Over-go – run away from, desert ('*A's over-gon his childern an' woife*')
Over-live – outlive, survive

P

Pack-man – pedlar, hawker
Paddy, throw a – throw a tantrum, be in a bad mood
Pancheon – large circular pan, generally earthenware
Peaked – wasted, emaciated by disease, or pinched by cold
Peart – lively, vigorous, brisk
Peeping and tooting – prying and spying
Perished – cold
Pingle – small enclosure of land
Pipkin – glazed earthenware saucepan
Plaggy bags – plastic bags
Plimmies – plimsolls
Poddywig – tadpole
Pottered – disturbed, perplexed
Pot-valiant – made bold by drink
Proggle – goad, poke
Proud tailor – the goldfinch
Puggy – dirty, grimy; also touchy or apt to take offence
Pull-back – a drawback

Q

Quality – gentry, great people, 'company'
Queechy – ailing, sickly, feeble
Quick-sticks – quickly, at once

Quigger – next to nothing (*'it's foive moile, as near as a quigger'*)
Quilt – to beat or thrash
Quocken – suffocate, choke
Quoil – haycock

R

Rack up – to break up (something)
Raff – a dissolute vagabond
Raffling – loose and worthless
Rain-bird – the green woodpecker
Raisty – rancid
Ramper – main road or turnpike
Ranter – to darn
Rash out – to break out in a sweat (applied to horses)
Ratchet – a rat-hole
Raum – to reach for with effort, stretch after
Reckling – the youngest or smallest in a litter or brood
Redder – one who parts combatants, an umpire or 'settler'
Ret – growth of weeds in a pond or river
Revel – stray and ramble ('revel about the fields')
Riddle – a coarse wire sieve
Rig-and-balk/rig-and-furrow – traditional ways of dividing ploughed land: '*The ridge and furrow shows that once the crooked plough / Turned up the grassy turf where oaks are rooted now*' (Drayton, Poly-Olbion, XIX)

Right-down – downright

Right-on – immediately, straightaway

Right-out – outright, completely

Rind-tabberer – woodpecker (or roind-tabberer) See *Tabber* page 25

Roozle – rouse violently (*'he roozled him out of his sleep'*)

S

Sahth – south

Sarmunt – sermon (*'Which was ye thinkin' on, Seth, the pretty preacher's face or her sarmunt?'* ADAM BEDE)

Scrat – scratch, struggle or scramble on (*'Scrats at his bit o' garden, and makes two potatoes grow i'stead o' one'*, ADAM BEDE)

Scrattle – scratch with a noise, also scramble on through difficulties

Scrinch – a little bit, a morsel (*'Gie's a scrinch.'*)

Sen – self

Sket – useless person

Slack – quench the thirst

Slithering – loitering

Snead – the long handle or shank of a scythe

Snib – snub, rebuke

Snow-in-harvest – a simile for any unwelcome thing or person

Snozy – comfortable

Snufty – touchy, contentious

Solid – grave, earnest
Souse – a slap or blow
Sowter – a wooden lid used to crush the whey out of the curds in cheese making
Spink – chaffinch
Spirtle – to sprinkle, splash
Splatheradab – a chatterer, gossip, scandal-monger
Splurther – confusion, nonsense, fuss
Squadsies – a truce term in children's games (e.g. said to avoid capture)
Staddle – hay laid out in wide rows, collected with a pitchfork
Stannel – kestrel (corruption of 'standgale' from resisting the wind)
Startups – gaiters
Stocky – impudent, saucy, restive
Strap – draw out the last milk when milking a cow
Suity – suitable
Swelking – sultry, hot
Swiggle – drink freely
Swithen – to shrivel

T

Tabber – tap, strike quickly with the feet
Tabs – ears

Tahn – town

Tawzy – tangled, knotted (e.g. applied to hair). Also *'all of a tazz'*.

Tedding – spreading out the grass cut by the scythe in haymaking

Thack – thatch

Thack and mortar – with all one's might

That (+ adjective/adverb) – so (*'Eh wur that poorly'*)

Theave – a ewe before bearing the first lamb

Theirn – theirs

Thiller – shaft-horse in ploughing

This here – this

These here – these

Throng – busy

Thurrow – furrow

Tidd – fond (*'the child's so tidd of her little brother'*)

Tiss up – to somersault, twist

Turmit – turnip

Twitchell – narrow passageway between houses

Twizzle – roundabout way (*'turns and twizzles'*)

U

Up-a-daisy – said to a child who falls down

Upstir – uproar, commotion

Us/uz – our (*'we 'ad us dinners'*)

Us-sen – ourselves

Utic – the whinchat (representing the bird's song)

Uvver – over. Also used to mean 'upper' in place names, such as 'Overseal', distinguished from the lower-lying 'Netherseal'

V

Vally – value

Vamp – part of boot or shoe covering the front of the foot

Varge – verge

Varmint – vermin

Varnish – grow fat (*'that horse'll varnish in the spring'*)

Varsal – universal

Vast – a great quantity or number (*'a vast o' people, a vast o' corn'*)

W

Wadgeock – diminutive of 'wadge', small quantity, bundle

Waffle – yap or bark as a small dog (*'you should git a little wafflin' doog'*)

Wake – an annual village feast, usually with a small fair

Washing-pegs – clothes pegs

Waver – to waive, postpone (*'Yo'd best weever it till middle dee.'*)

Weezeling – giddiness

Well made up – pleased

Werrish – feeble, of a delicate constitution

Westy – giddy, confused

Whiffle – whisk (said of the wind, e.g. *'the wind whiffling the snow'*)

Whingeling – whining and pining

Widdle – move loosely about, oscillate (like a rope)

Windflower – wood anemone

Wittering – wearisome, tedious

Wizzle – weasel

Wool-stapler – wool merchant

Wull – will

Yack – throw

Yaffle – yelp, yap like a dog

Yer – you, you are

Yetters – 'yet-wise', yet (*'I've not been up there yetters'*)

Yo – you

Yoller – yellow

Yonaway – in that direction

Yorp – talk boisterously

Yorn – yours

Yowl – howl, yell

An Early Account of Leicestershire Dialect

The History and Antiquities of Claybrook by the REV. A. MACAULAY, published in 1791, contains an interesting passage (reproduced here in modern print) describing some of the characteristics of the dialect of ordinary folk in that village at the time – as represented, that is, through the spelling in Macaulay's examples:

The dialect of the common people, though broad, is sufficiently plain and intelligible. They have a strong propensity to aspirate their words; the letter H comes in almost on every occasion where it ought not, and is as frequently omitted where it ought to come in. The words 'FINE', 'MINE', and such like, are pronounced as if they were spelt 'FOINE', 'MOINE'; 'PLACE', 'FACE', etc., as if they were spelt 'PLEACE', 'FEACE', and in the plural sometimes you hear 'PLEACEN'; 'CLOSEN' for 'CLOSES'; and many other words in the same style of Saxon termination. The words 'THERE' and 'WHERE' are generally pronounced thus, 'THEERE', 'WHEERE'; the words 'MERCY', 'DESERVE', etc., thus, 'MARCY', 'DESARVE'. The following peculiarities of pronunciation are likewise observable: 'UZ', strongly aspirated, for 'US', 'WAR' for 'WAS', 'MEED' for 'MAID', 'FAITHER' for 'FATHER', 'E'ERY' for 'EVERY', 'BRIG' for 'BRIDGE', 'THURROUGH' for 'FURROW', 'HAWF' for 'HALF', 'CART-RIT' for 'RUT', 'MALEFACTORY' for 'MANUFACTORY', 'INACTIOUS' for 'ANXIOUS'. The words 'MYSEN' and 'HIMSEN' are sometimes used instead of 'MYSELF' and 'HIMSELF'; the word 'SHACK' is used to denote an idle, worthless vagabond; and the word 'RIP' one who is very profane.

Some Place Names and What They Tell Us

As one of the most diverse and vibrant cities in the country, Leicester has a character all its own, created by the cultural richness of its past as well as its present. The earliest settlers in the area were of Celtic origin, people of the *Corieltauvi tribe*, who were able to cross the River Soar here. For the Romans, similarly, it was a strategic place to establish a garrison which developed into a town they called *Ratae*. Although in a remote part of the Roman Empire, *Ratae* had a bath-house and other public buildings, and examples of the Romans' decorative workmanship can be seen in the mosaic pavements displayed in the Jewry Wall Museum.

After the Romans left, Saxon culture gradually established itself. The name LEICESTER comes from *Ligoracester* in Anglo-Saxon, which means fortified town of the *Ligore*, the ancient river name adopted by the early Celtic settlers for themselves. The River Soar is called the *Leir* on some old maps, based on that Celtic name, and interestingly the Welsh name for Leicester is *Caer Lyr'*

The influence of Viking rule (the area fell within the Danelaw) is clearly seen in place names in the East Midlands. A number of street names in Leicester ending in *'Gate'*, such as *Church Gate* and *Gallowtree Gate*, are derived from *gata*, the Danish word for road. Many places in Leicestershire end in *–by* (*Oadby, Enderby, Thurnby,* etc.), which is the Viking word for farm, and these tended originally to be on relatively poor ground – *Thurnby*, for example, means *a farm on thorny land*. Viking farmsteads are also indicated by the word *thorpe*, as in Ullesthorpe or Bruntingthorpe. Names ending this way often had the variations *thrupp* or *trup,* as in *Wollesthorpe*, pronounced locally as 'Woolstrup'. Some places have hybrid names, combining a Viking personal name with the Anglo-Saxon ending *tun*, such as *Thrussington*, meaning the village of the Dane THORSTEINN. Viking farmsteads are also indicated by the name *Thorpe*, as in *Thorpe Langton*. Names ending in –*thorp* often had the variations *–thrupp* or *–trup*, for example *Wollesthorpe*, pronounced locally as *Woolstrup*.

The next group of people to leave their mark on Leicester were the Normans, who arrived after the BATTLE OF HASTINGS in 1066. The Norman barons had considerable power and wealth and built the Church of ST MARY DE CASTRO around 1107 and the castle complex. Some of their names are preserved in place names like *Ashby de la Zouch* and *Melton Mowbray*. *Goadby Marwood* goes back to the family name *Maureward*, while *Burton Overy's* spelling conceals its real origins: *Burton Noveray*.

The ending *–worth* refers to a settlement. The name *Kibworth* means the *estate of Cybba*, an Anglo-Saxon lord. After the Norman Conquest the two parts of this village became *Kibworth Beauchamp* and *Kibworth Harcourt*, adding the names of their respective Norman lords.

The village of *Husbands Bosworth* started out as *Baresworde* (probably *Bar's settlement* or *farm*). Later, to distinguish it from *Market Bosworth*, the word *'Husbandmen's'* was added, which showed it was the smaller, farming village. Not surprisingly, having become quite a tongue twister, the name was soon simplified to the version it has today.

An old legend (undoubtedly concocted by someone who enjoyed wordplay) about a giant called BEL is associated with the placenames *Mountsorrel*, *Wanlip*, *Burstall* and *Belgrave*. The story goes that BEL vowed he would reach Leicester from *Mountsorrel* in three leaps. So he 'mounted' his 'sorrel' horse at *Mountsorrel*. Then 'one leap' carried him safely to *Wanlip*, but on attempting a second leap he 'burst all' – his harness, horse and himself – at *Burstall*. Despite this misfortune, he attempted a third leap, but both horse and rider dropped dead a mile and a half short of Leicester and were buried together at *'Belgrave'*.

Quite a few place names in the city and county are not pronounced as you would expect from their spelling. In earlier days *Thurcaston, Thurlaston* and *Thurmaston* were known locally as *Throoks'n, Throols'n* and *Throoms'n*. *Belvoir* is pronounced *'beaver'*. *Coalville* often loses its first *'l'* and sounds like *'Coa'ville'*. *Grace Dieu* is pronounced like *'Gracedew'*, and *Groby* is actually *'Grooby'* (spellings in the past have made this clearer than it is now). These are just a few of the traps waiting for the uninitiated visitor or traveller who asks for directions.

A few landmarks in the city and its surroundings have acquired unusual names. *The Pork Pie Chapel* in *Belvoir Street* was built in 1845 as a United Baptist Chapel. It was designed by JOSEPH HANSOM, who also designed the *New Walk Museum* and the Hansom cab. The ruin in *Bradgate Park* known as *Old John* was built in 1786 by the EARL OF STAMFORD in memory of a retainer named John who apparently liked his ale. So the resemblance to a beer mug is, allegedly, no coincidence! The retainer John met an untimely death, incidentally, when a maypole fell on him at a coming of age celebration for the Earl's grandson.

Old John on a Winter's Day iStock

Richard III

Today's bustling, multicultural city of more than 300,000 people is a very different place from the medieval town of Leicester at the time of the BATTLE OF BOSWORTH in 1485. However, the discovery and identification of the mortal remains of KING RICHARD III in a car park in the city in August 2012 suddenly brought that dramatic time in Leicester's past to the whole world's attention. The car park in question had been built over what had once been the site of a medieval Franciscan friary of the GREY FRIARS, where the king was hastily buried two days after his death. Before the battle he slept in the BLUE BOAR INN where, according to some accounts, he left his royal bed. He was apparently confident and smiling the following day as he rode with an army of thousands to battle, little imagining that day would be his last. After his defeat his naked, battered and abused body was brought back to Leicester slung over a horse and laid out for public view at The Newarke for two days.

The king's mortal remains were reinterred with great dignity at Leicester Cathedral in March 2015, and the spot where they were rediscovered is now within the KING RICHARD III VISITOR CENTRE. There you can learn much more about all aspects of this amazing discovery.

King Richard III last of the Plantagenets
iStock

Village Life and Customs

The Whipping Toms

This was an ancient custom once associated with the Newarke in Leicester. On Shrove Tuesday people flocked to a large open space at this spot to enjoy games in the morning. In the afternoon strong men called Whipping Toms would chase and cart-whip anyone wishing to pass through the Newarke unless they paid them a fee. A bell was rung to announce their arrival, and those they chased would try to defend themselves robustly with sticks. The Whipping Toms were not permitted to whip above the knee, and any person who knelt down could not be whipped as long as they stayed in that position. The custom was brought to an end in the middle of the 19th century by means of a clause in a so-called *'Leicester Improvement Act'* passed in 1846.

Hallaton Bottle Kicking

One of the most exciting and eccentric village customs to have survived the centuries is the famous hare-pie scramble and bottle kicking held on Easter Monday in the village of Hallaton. The bottle kicking involves competition against rivals from the neighbouring village of Medbourne. Though written records go back only to the late 18th century, the custom is thought to have originated in medieval times. What we know from the records is that the village rector was bequeathed some land called *'Hare-crop-leys'* on condition that he and succeeding rectors provided *'two hare pies, a quantity of ale, and two dozen penny loaves, to be scrambled for'* every year on *'Hare Pie Bank'*, a short distance south of the village. Actually, since hares are out of season for eating at this time, they have traditionally been substituted by other meats. One rector around 1790 wanted to put the funds 'to better use', but not surprisingly gave up on the idea when his house and the church were daubed with the slogan *No pie, no parson, and a job for the glazier.*

In both Hallaton and Medbourne the day begins with a parade. In Hallaton there is a procession from The Fox Inn led by the Warrener carrying a staff with the figure of a hare on the top. Attendants carry baskets of bread and the Hare Pie. Part of the pie is cut up and thrown to the crowd for the *'scramble'*, while the rest is placed in a sack and carried later to Hare Pie Bank. Three bottles (actually small barrels or kegs) are taken to the Buttercross on the village green to be dressed with ribbons. In the afternoon a parade departs to the bottle-kicking field. Before the bottle kicking begins the hare pie is spread on the ground at the top of the bank. Then each bottle is tossed three times as a signal to start the competition. The rival teams of Hallaton and Medbourne (and anyone else brave enough to take part) then have to try to move the bottles across streams, hedges and any other obstacles to their own village. The winners celebrate with copious quantities of ale in the village pubs.

Hallaton – Hare Pie Ceremony Imageleicestershire.org

Wakes and Festivals

Traditionally, every village in the county would hold an annual feast, generally on the day of its patron saint. Hiring fairs were also held, usually in the autumn following harvest, where workers could meet potential employers and they could discuss working conditions and pay. If they were promised work, they would be given a small advance of wages called *earnest money*. A worker could go to fairs in other parts of Leicestershire or to a neighbouring county, such as Warwickshire, if he or she failed to find work.

On Shrove Tuesday, when churches would ring a *'Pancake Bell'* at midday as a signal for people to start frying their pancakes, schoolchildren would enjoy a free afternoon to play games like shuttlecock and battledore. In Frisby-on-the-Wreake, there was a custom called *barring the master out of school*. When the Pancake Bell rang, the pupils would entice their teacher outside and then lock the door. They would then chant:

Pardon, master, pardon,
Pardon in a pin,
If you don't give a holiday,
We won't let you in.

Roy Palmer (1985) tells us that another festival, **Plough Monday**, was celebrated in many villages on the first Monday after *Twelfth Day* (6 January). Ploughmen went from house to house collecting money, food and drink. In different places they were called *morris dancers, plough bullockers, plough boys* or *molly guizers*. They disguised themselves by painting their faces black or red and by donning extravagant costumes. Because they made themselves unrecognisable they often appeared menacing and frightened local people. In Markfield they would drag a plough through the streets and, for devilment, sometimes plough up lawns and paths. Their songs and chants would usually have the effect of encouraging instant contributions at the door, like this song from *Woodhouse Eaves*:

Tramp, tramp, tramp the boys are marching,
Cheer up, the boys are at your door.
If you do not let us in
We will kick the door in.
And you won't see your mother any more.

Thomas Page and the Smallpox 'Scam'

In Macaulay's *History of Claybrook* we find the delightful story of THOMAS PAGE. Through misfortune Page was forced to sell his landed property, which was bought by a magistrate called MR BYRD, known as *'The Old Justice'*. In return Byrd agreed to provide an annuity to Page's wife if she outlived him. Soon after this, Page left the village for London, leaving his wife in Claybrook. Shortly official news came that he had died there of smallpox and been buried in St Pancras churchyard. Page's widow then claimed her money. However, one day Mr Byrd spotted a letter in Lutterworth addressed to the 'Widow of Claybrook'. The handwriting made him curious, to say the least, so he opened it and discovered it was from none other than Thomas Page, who was, it now seemed, very much alive and well.

Determined to investigate, Byrd went to London and had Page's coffin disinterred, only to discover it contained merely stones and wool. Page was later caught and sent to prison but released after a short time and allowed to return as a pauper to Claybrook. Not surprisingly, his scam became a source of much humour after this. When there was an outbreak of smallpox in the village and Page expressed worries about having possible symptoms, a local farmer asked him wryly why he, of all people in the parish, should be so afraid, since everyone knew he had already died of the disease many years earlier! Page responded: *'Well, come now, warn't that a good cunning trick as I sarved the old Justice'*. *'Yes'*, replied the farmer, *'no doubt it would have been a very good trick indeed – if it had succeeded, Master Page!'*

Farming and Food

The agriculturalist ROBERT BAKEWELL (1725–95), born in Dishley, revolutionised sheep and cattle farming through the use of selective breeding methods that are still followed today. His Leicester sheep produced long coarse wool and high-quality meat. Daniel Defoe, who travelled through the county in the 18th century, commented: '*The sheep bred in this county are, without comparison, the largest, and bear not only the greatest weight of flesh on their bones, but also the greatest fleece of wool on their backs of any sheep of England*'.

Robert Bakewell on a bay cob Imageleicestershire.org

To the non-specialist the names traditionally given to sheep of different ages are quite bewildering. Lambs had that name until the time of 'going to turnips' in the autumn, after which they were called tegs until their first shearing. After that they could be called not only tegs but also hogs, hoggets, hoggrels, shear-hogs or shearlings, with the females having the additional name of theaves. After the second shearing they lost the name tegs but retained the other names and acquired the additional name two-shears. Females could sometimes be called double-theaves. After the third shearing the males were called wethers and the females ewes. I wonder how many of these names are still in use by sheep farmers today.

A Leicestershire sheep Imageleicestershire.org

It's all too easy to forget nowadays that farmers were dependent on horses in the past to manage the heavier work on the land. The wagoner or ploughman had quite an extensive set of terms to use with a team of horses, including *Hayt!* (to the thiller or horse in the shafts) for *'go over to the off side'*, and *Come over!* or *Come ether!* (to the fore-horse) for *'come over to the near side'*. *Way!* or *Wo!* was said for halting and *Gee back!* for going backwards. For entering the stable the usual greeting was *Soo, so-oo!*, while *Gently! Stan'!* and *Wo-hey!* would be said during grooming. The most frequent names for farm horses were CAPTAIN, GILBERT, DOBBIN, DUKE, DAISY, BETTY or DUCHESS. GILBERT was usually a chestnut. A dappled grey would usually be called DUMPLING and a roan STRAWBERRY.

Red Leicester

Red Leicester, a cheese originally made on small farms, got its distinctive orange colour from a dye created from an extract of carrots. It was used in many traditional cottage recipes, such as Leicestershire Rarebit, which was made by toasting bread and soaking it in beer and red wine. It was then covered with a slice of the cheese and placed in front of the fire to melt the cheese.

Stilton

Known as the 'king of cheeses', **Stilton's** history goes back to the early 18th century. It takes its name from the village of Stilton in Cambridgeshire, where it was first made and sold (then as a pressed, cooked, cream cheese), but it then evolved in Leicestershire into the semi-hard blue-vein cheese we know today. Blue or White Stilton both have protected status and can only be produced in the three counties of Derbyshire, Nottinghamshire and Leicestershire. Only six dairies in the whole world are licensed to make the cheese and between them they make over a million Stilton cheeses a year. According to a 19th-century saying, 'if you drink a pot of ale and eat a scoop of Stilton every day, you will make "old bones"'.

Stilton is delicious with pears. Try this quick savoury snack: toast a slice of bread on both sides, top it with some chopped watercress, a sliced pear and then a slice of Stilton. Sprinkle with cayenne pepper and bake for five minutes. Stilton is also the traditional cheese eaten with a glass of port.

Melton Mowbray pork pies

Dickinson and Morris have been making their famous pork pies since 1851 at *'Ye Olde Pork Pie Shoppe'* in Melton Mowbray. The fox hunting gentry, with whom these pies were very popular, helped to spread their fame, and the connection of the Midland Line railway to King's Cross, London, also meant they could be sold far and wide. In the 1990s, high demand led to major supermarkets also stocking Melton Mowbray pies. Today, baking takes place at a bakery outside Leicester as well as in the shop in Melton Mowbray.

Bosworth Jumbles

Legend has it that some of these small cakes were dropped from the pocket of King Richard III's cook on Bosworth battlefield.

THIS IS HOW YOU MAKE THEM:

Cream 6 oz butter and 6 oz sugar together until light and fluffy. Beat in an egg and some grated lemon rind. Then sieve in 8oz flour and mix to a stiff consistency.

Divide the mixture into small pieces. These should be shaped like an 'S' before baking for 20 minutes on a greased baking tray.

Oven: 350°F/180°C Gas Mark 4

Work and Industry

Framework knitting

The framework knitter operated the treadles with both feet and had to move the iron carriage on its wooden frame with both arms. Men would usually operate the frame and women would seam the stockings while children wound yarn onto bobbins.

Framework knitting
Imageleicestershire.org

Although the knitters often worked on a frame in their own cottages they were far from being independent workers and their lives became very hard through poverty. 'As poor as a stockinger' (another name for framework knitter) was a common expression. Most had to pay rent to a middleman or master (also given names like putter out, undertaker, bag hosier or bagman) who supplied them with frames (owned by hosiers) and yarn for stockings, gloves and other items. The knitters would have to pay the rent even when they were ill or the frame was not in use.

PALMER (1985) quotes a very telling song of 1854:

The Middleman's a docking man,
A constant peace destroyer,
A warehouse rat that digs between
The employed and the employer.

The Middleman's a useless man,
He is not worth a tester;
An' the sooner he becomes defunct
The better for old Leicester.

The conditions of the framework knitters were particularly severe when fashions changed and men began to wear trousers rather than knee-breeches. This meant a drop in demand for long stockings. Poverty drove some weavers to violent action and in 1811 frames were attacked and destroyed in numerous places. In 1816 serious disturbances in Loughborough, where both knitting frames and lace-making machines were smashed, resulted in several of the attackers being tried and hanged in Leicester. Improvements came only gradually as the organisation of the hosiery industry changed for the better.

The Corah brothers built a knitwear factory in Leicester in 1865. Their steam-powered knitting machines considerably reduced the cost of making stockings, and other factories soon followed. Frame rents were abolished in the 1870s and Education Acts came into force, making schooling compulsory until the age of ten. Knitters were no longer able to use their young children as general helpers, so the cottage workshops gradually came to an end. It took time, though, for stockingers to get used to the supervised and regimented life of factory hands and for their conditions to improve, for example through the provision of recreational facilities as well as increased wages. In the latter half of the 19th century Leicester became more prosperous as new industries also played their part, such as glove-making and, in particular, the manufacturing of boots and shoes.

Early schools

In the 1870s entries in the school log book by the headmaster of Albert Road Board School in Hinckley reveal that children were frequently away from class. Sadly, this was often because of contagious diseases or insufficient clothing and footwear in bad weather. Entries for March 1895 report two deaths among the pupils from diphtheria, and through to the 1900s numerous entries refer to absences caused by measles, ringworm and whooping cough. However, on happier occasions children missed school to attend circuses or other festivities in the community. In one entry for

October 1874, we find the following summary:

> *Attendance low today; a menagerie in the town and holiday for stockingers which has kept a number of children at home (Elverstone 2014: 14)*

Classroom with children at desks Imageleicestershire.org

An earlier school, the Old Grammar School built in 1614 in Market Harborough to provide education for the poor, was erected on stilts so that the butter market could be held under it, keeping the traders dry in foul weather. The school was built with funds set up by a great benefactor from the town, Robert Smyth. He was the son of a poor tailor who made his fortune in London and became

Controller to the Lord Mayor's Court and a member of the influential Merchant Taylor's Guild. It remained in use as a school until 1892. Today it is one of the town's best-known historical buildings and occasional stalls still sell flowers and other items beneath it. The Old Grammar School has now become a much-loved symbol of the town's history.

Children's games

Some traditional playground games that were enjoyed by children in Leicestershire in the past include **Duck Stone** and **Up the needle and down the thread**.

In the game of **Duck Stone**, typically played by boys, a large stone had a small stone placed on top of it, which the player would try to topple by throwing a third stone at it. If successful, he would run and try to pick up his own stone in his cap, without touching it. At the same time his opponent would try to replace the small stone and 'tig' the thrower before he could get back to base.

Up the needle and down the thread would be played by girls standing in a line, each holding the girl in front by the waist. The line would process round the playground until it reached a wall. The girl at the front would then place one hand on the wall, forming an arch for the rest of the line to pass through. The leader would then run to the back of the line and the second girl would take over until all had been leader in turn.

Symington's and the Liberty Bodice

Two brothers from Scotland, JAMES and WILLIAM SYMINGTON, opened factories in Market Harborough in the 19th century. William was a grocer at first but soon developed *'Symington's Soups'*, which became a household name. James worked as a draper and tailor before starting to manufacture undergarments. Symington's Corsets had a purpose-built factory in Adam and Eve Street, and today this building houses the Harborough District Council offices as well as the Library, Tourist Information Centre and Harborough Museum.

Square and Corset Factory Imageleicestershire.org

Symingtons expanded in the last century and by the 1930s was also producing a range of swimwear. During the Second World War they were called upon to make parachutes. By 1967, when they became part of the Courtauld group after a steady decline in the post-war market, they had factories and operations in five countries.

The Symington's 'Liberty Bodice', designed by FREDERICK COX and modelled by his daughter FREDA, became a widely known and highly successful product. It was a light, fleecy vest of cotton wool with woven tapes running down the garment, less constricting for the female figure than a stiff corset, and stockings and underwear could be buttoned on to it. Millions were sold in the 1930s and production was to go on for more than sixty years.

An original Liberty Bodice, 1908
Imageleicestershire.org

Here, Mr Gilbert, who worked at the Symington factory, recalls the factory buzzer and the way money was taken to the bank:

> *... they blew a big buzzer at five to eight ... terrific noise you could 'ear it all over 'arborough ... that were at foive to eight yer see and they'd all be p'raps standin' outside readin' the papers, smokin' and when that went they'd all gradually [go inside]*
>
> *I tell yer what ... how they used to fetch the money from 'ere. I mean there were ... what ... two thousand girls worked here I'll bet ... oh yes, must've been two thousand ... they used to fetch it in a barrer [barrow] ... two men that's all ... must've been a few pound at that time ... they used to fetch it in this barrer ... and cross to the bank there ... whether they were armed or not I never knew...*

[transcribed from the audio archive of Harborough Museum – MH-013-1]

Footwear Manufacturing

Like Northampton, Leicester was well known as a boot- and shoe-making city. Leaders of the industry in the mid-1800s were THOMAS CRICK of Peacock Lane and J. DILKES of Loseby Lane. By 1843 a number of shoemakers were selling ready-made boots in so-called 'show shops' in the city, and by 1871 the number of workers employed in making boots and shoes was around eleven thousand. The well-known shoe company Stead and Simpson established their headquarters in the city, not only manufacturing but selling their footwear through a chain of shops.

Something we take absolutely for granted today is that when we buy a pair of shoes there will be a left and a right shoe, but until the 1780s shoes were made for either foot, which we can well imagine was not half as comfortable or snug a fit.

Heel Building and Attaching Imageleicestershire.org

An example of a family-run footwear manufacturer elsewhere in the county was Falkner's of Market Harborough, which was in operation from the 1830s till

1986. Boots and shoes for regular clients would be made using their personal lasts, which were carefully stored in readiness. A replica of the firm's workroom with its original tools and fittings can be visited in Harborough Museum.

Here Mr William Falkner recalls how his family firm made riding boots for the local Fernie Hunt supporters;

> *... well yes the Fer ... we used to supply the Fernie and er ... well ... in the ... up in those old records you know we got the drawin's of the feet round there and er ... yeah they were sought after ... I 'ad somebody in the other day oh she said we made 'er father a pair and I said yeah they were good boots ... we still got those two on exhibition like.* [transcribed from the audio archive of Harborough Museum – MH-083-a]

Coal Mining

Mining goes back a very long time in Leicestershire, as it does in Nottinghamshire. Pits were recorded in the 13th century at Donington-le-Heath, Swannington and Worthington, and in the 14th century at Staunton Harold. Miners have always been a close-knit community with many distinctive terms and expressions associated with their work and equipment. They would greet each other with the phrase 'old bud' (bird) and would say 'drawing out the wood' for pulling out the pit props and to 'shirt it' for stopping work at the end of a shift. They used a snap-tin for their snap or lunch and carried a dudley or tin for holding about a quart of water. They called the part of the mine left abandoned after the coal had been extracted 'the gob'.

The dialect of the mining communities in the East Midlands in the early 20th century was vividly represented by the Nottinghamshire writer D.H. LAWRENCE. Here is an extract from his short story *'Odour of Chrysanthemums'*, published in 1914, in which a miner's wife, Elizabeth, waits increasingly anxiously when her husband fails to come home from his shift at the mine. Her elderly mother-in-law is now with her and the children have been sent to bed. Someone eventually comes to the door:

It was a man in pit-clothes.

'They're bringin' 'im, Missis,' he said. Elizabeth's heart halted a moment. Then it surged on again, almost suffocating her.

'Is he – is it bad?' she asked.

The man turned away, looking at the darkness.

'The doctor says 'e'd been dead hours. 'E saw 'im i' th' lamp-cabin.'

The old woman, who stood just behind Elizabeth, dropped into a chair, and folded her hands, crying: 'Oh, my boy, my boy!'

'Hush!' said Elizabeth, with a sharp twitch of a frown. 'Be still, mother, don't waken th' children: I wouldn't have them down for anything!'

The old woman moaned softly, rocking herself. The man was drawing away. Elizabeth took a step forward.
'How was it?' she asked.
'Well, I couldn't say for sure,' the man replied, very ill at ease. 'E wor finishin' a stint an' th' butties 'ad gone, an' a lot o' stuff come down atop 'n 'im.'

Mining is dangerous work, and miners were known to be superstitious. Seeing a woman or a parson on the way to the pit was apparently considered a bad omen. In Leicestershire there were few major mining disasters, though in 1898 in the Whitwick colliery 35 miners died as a result of an underground fire. They left behind 27 widows and 84 children under thirteen.

Place Rhymes and Local Sayings

A weather saying:
If the wind's i' the East of Easter-dee,
Yo'll ha' plenty o' grass, but little good hee. [i.e. hay]

We must dew as the'
Dew at Quorn
What we don't dew to dee,
We must dew i' the morn'.

When a doys thee'll ba wet oys i' Grewby Pule.

(When he dies there'll be wet eyes in Groby Pool – sarcastic, meaning that no one will cry for him. Presumably the fish in 'Grewby Pule' already have wet eyes!)

If that happens then I'll thatch Groby Pool with pancakes.

(said of something that is highly improbable)

He's gone over Asfordby bridge backwards.

(he's put the cart before the horse)

He'd never stop a pig in a passage.

(said of a bow-legged man)

EVERY REGION HAS ITS TRADITIONAL PUT-DOWNS AND INSULTS, SOME OF THEM INVOLVING PLACE NAMES. HERE'S A PUBLISHABLE ONE:

Put up your pipes, and go to Lockington Wake!

(the equivalent of 'get lost!' – Lockington being in a remote corner of the county)

The term *'bean belly Leicestershire'* comes from a rhyme in MICHAEL DRAYTON'S *Poly-Olbion*:

Bean belly Leicestershire, her attribute doth bear.
And bells and bagpipes next, belong to Lincolnshire.

There was a saying that if you shook a Leicestershire yeoman by the collar, you would hear the beans rattle in his belly.

Barton-in-the-Beans village sign
iStock

Many early rhymes about villages reveal local rivalries and allegiances that are, perhaps, still remembered and felt today:

Mountsorrel is a stony place;
Sileby it be sandy.
Rothley has the Half-Way house;
Quorndon is the dandy.

Fox Hunting and Horse Racing

Leicestershire is considered the home of the traditional sport of fox hunting – in fact the fox is the emblem of the county council, and Leicester City Football Club are known as *'The Foxes'*. The most famous packs of foxhounds of the 19th century are still familiar names today: THE BELVOIR, THE COTTESMORE, THE QUORN, THE FERNIE and THE PYTCHLEY. Each had its own 'country' and the thrills and spills of the chase were always guaranteed by the many challenging natural obstacles that had to be jumped.

Hundreds of horses were stabled at Melton Mowbray for the hunting season, which started in November. The town was the main centre of both the sport and the social life around it, and royalty and aristocrats were regular visitors during the hunting season, usually owning large houses known as 'Hunting Boxes'. An infamous event took place in Melton in April 1837 when the Marquis of Waterford and his friends, after a night's drinking at a Hunt Ball, went on the rampage through the town, breaking toll gates and daubing red paint on The White Swan, shop fronts and even people! This is the source of the expression 'painting the town red'. Their social status ensured that, although apprehended and brought before Derby Assizes, they were not found guilty of riot but given only what would have been for them a modest fine.

The population of Melton rose from 2,000 to 15,000 during the 19th century, largely because of the growth in employment supporting the hunts and catering for their followers. However, huntsmen were not universally popular and the apparently arrogant behaviour of some 'noble gentlemen' shows the great social gulf between them and more 'humble folk' at the time.

Victorian foxhunting scene iStock

The heyday of fox hunting was reached in the inter-war years of the last century, when it provided a substantial input to the rural economy. Although it is now illegal to use dogs to kill foxes, hunts still meet for the excitement of riding together cross country. They lay scent trails in advance and the sport is now usually called 'drag hunting'.

Horse racing has always been popular in the county and in Leicester dates back to 1603. There was annual racing in September on Abbey Meadow, but both that course and a subsequent one in St Mary's Field were at risk of being flooded by the River Soar. In 1804 the racecourse was moved to Victoria Park and a mile-long track was used there until 1883, when the Oadby racecourse in use today was opened. Some towns in the county also had their own racecourses, including Loughborough, Oakham and Uppingham.

One colourful character who promoted steeplechasing in the county was BENEDICT JOHN ANGELL, better known as *Jack 'Cherry' Angell*, who lived in Tower House in Lubenham. The nickname *'Cherry'* came from the impressive phaeton coach he owned, which was made of cherry-wood. He and his friends organised the first National Hunt Chase Challenge Cup in 1860, which was run in Farndon Fields and won by Cherry's own horse, Bridegroom. Whenever his horses won a major race, he would apparently celebrate by adding a new room to his house. The tall tower that was to give the house its name was built when his horse Alcibade won the Grand National in 1865. This structure gave the village a striking new landmark and Cherry an excellent view of his horses in training.

Canals

For thirty years or more canals were the main means of transporting coal and other bulk cargoes. The Grand Union Canal links London to Birmingham and is our longest canal, with several branch lines. It was constructed through the 'union' of several independent waterways, of which the oldest were the navigations around the River Soar.

Foxton Locks, on the Leicester Line, can be found a few miles south west of Market Harborough and is one of Leicestershire's top visitor attractions. A staircase of ten locks rising 75 feet (23m), it was completed in 1812. An original plan to take the canal beyond Harborough towards Northampton to join the London to Birmingham canal was abandoned due to projected costs. A south-westward route was then chosen instead, which involved the building of the lock stairway, and the connection was completed in 1814. The 'Harborough Arm' was soon used by local traders to transport goods around the area, particularly coal and corn, since the canal boats could carry much heavier loads and were more economical to run than stagecoaches. Over the years this stretch has always been used for pleasure boating and for walking along the towpath and has remained a popular extension of the Grand Union, leading today to a colourful wharf full of narrowboats overlooked by stylish canalside properties in converted warehouses.

It takes about three-quarters of an hour for a canal boat to pass up or down the lock stairway. To save time an experimental inclined plane was constructed at the turn of the 20th century, allowing boats to be lifted up and down the incline instead of going through the locks, but this was not a lasting success and eventually fell into disuse. It is still possible to see where the inclined plane was and there are plans to restore it.

These days Foxton Locks is a unique and fascinating attraction and both locals and tourists can spend hours watching the process of lock opening and closing, visiting the Canal Museum and enjoying refreshments at the Foxton Locks Inn overlooking the canal basin.

Foxton Locks iStock

This sobering anecdote from a glossary of 1881 was used to illustrate the word 'navigation' but also represents through non-standard spelling the dialect pronunciation of a number of other words associated with the canals:

'Run, John', she says, 'the masster's hulled his-sen i' the navigeetion,' she says. Soo ah runs up the bank by th'akedok, an' muster Coaly, a wur a-runnin' alung the too-path, an' a says, 'Theer's a man i' the canell,' a says, 'an' ah thenk it's muster Godfrey.' Soo way coom an' got 'im out o' the cut after a bit, but a wur quoite dead by then.'

The Great War

Here is a First World War soldier, FRED TUFTS, one of the *'Harborough Boys'* who served in the Leicestershire Regiment, describing his memories of the trenches:

I s'll always remember the first time I went into the trenches [...] we marched onto a field just ouside Loca [?] for a drum-'ead service ... and the Lincoln band ... we took the Lincoln band out with us ... the Leicester band din't go out [...] 'ey were made stretcher bearers ... the Lincoln band went out and I remember 'em playing I remember the old 'ymn 'Oh God Our 'elp in Ages Past' and we were just goin' up the bloomin' trenches one Sunday night we din't know what were in front of us you know but it were pretty quiet ...

bullets goin' about … 'ad bullets but nothin' … it was very quiet … we were a good way up to the trenches as well … going up in the dark you gorra keep in touch with the man in front of yer else yer lose contact you know.

[Extract from audio archive of Harborough Museum]

After the war, Fred Tufts returned to Harborough and resumed his former employment at Symington's, retiring 49 years later.

There is an important connection between the Great War and the University of Leicester. The idea of establishing a university in the city had been talked about as early as the 1880s, and before the end of the First World War it was suggested that such an institution would be a fitting 'living memorial' to those who had lost their lives. A fund was established and local textile manufacturer THOMAS FIELDING JOHNSON bought the old asylum building in 1919 for use as a University College. The first students were admitted in 1921, and the University of Leicester was granted its Royal Charter in 1957. The University's motto Ut Vitam Habeant (*'so that they may have life'*) reminds us of how it came to be founded.

In 1925 the imposing Cenotaph War Memorial by Sir Edwin Lutyens, famous for designing the Cenotaph in Whitehall in London, was also built in Victoria Park, on the edge of today's university campus.

Some Leicestershire Notables from the Past

Simon de Montfort (1208–65) was the 6th Earl of Leicester. He led a revolt against Henry III with a council of barons who established the first English Parliament. He was killed in battle against the king in 1265. The city has honoured his memory on several occasions, naming a concert hall, square, street and its second university after him.

Lady Jane Grey (1537–54) lived at Bradgate Park near Newtown Linford. She had royal blood, as one of the great-nieces of Henry VIII, and married a nobleman, Lord Guilford Dudley, the son of the Duke of Northumberland. On the death of Edward VI in 1553 she became embroiled in a plot engineered by the Duke to have her claim the throne and thereby further his own power and influence. She was duly proclaimed queen, only to be deposed by her cousin Mary Tudor, who had retained the support of the people. She was found guilty of treason and, along with her husband, was beheaded on Tower Hill. According to a local tradition, the oak trees in Bradgate Park were pollarded as a sign of mourning when she was executed. She is known as the 'Nine Day Queen'.

DANIEL LAMBERT (1770–1809), or 'Danny' as he was known, has gone down in history for his extraordinary size. After reaching his teens at normal weight, he started to put on the pounds dramatically and, by the time of his death, it was thought he weighed around 57 stones. He was a good swimmer and sang well, but the Victorian age was not averse to exhibiting people as curiosities and he was forced to earn money by putting himself on show in Piccadilly, London. He spent his final years partly in Leicester and died suddenly in Stamford, where he had gone to watch the races, at the age of 39. Some of his possessions, including his chair and clothes, are displayed in the Newarke Houses Museum in Leicester.

JOSEPH CAREY MERRICK (1862–90) became even more famous because of his unusual appearance. When he was a small child Merrick's face swelled inexplicably, his feet and right arm became enlarged and he was left lame after a fall. Not being cared for properly and unable to work normally, he finally allowed himself to be exhibited by a group of people who put on fairs. He was to suffer terrible neglect in the course of his life, but it seems he was eventually treated sympathetically and given more support as opponents of 'freak shows' began to influence public attitudes. The 1980 film *The Elephant Man*, directed by DAVID LYNCH and with JOHN HURT in the main role, tells his remarkable story.

Although originally from Melbourne in Derbyshire, **THOMAS COOK** (the great travel pioneer) spent ten years of his life in Market Harborough. He organised the first train excursion from Leicester in July 1841, a day trip to Loughborough and back. The fare of one shilling was good value for money, even including afternoon tea! Cook had been a cabinet-maker and was also a former Baptist preacher who believed, as a supporter of the Temperance Movement, that many of the social ills of his time could be overcome if people turned away from alcohol and were better educated. While walking from Market Harborough to Leicester one day in June 1841 he considered, as he recalled later, 'the practicability of employing the great powers of railways and locomotion for the furtherance of this social reform'. In 1850 there was a day trip to Ashby de la Zouch which promised in its advertisement visits to grand buildings, and in addition 'a variety of Popular Amusements, including Cricket, Archery, Skittles, Quoits, etc., with one or more Quadrille Bands'.

LEICESTER CITY FOOTBALL CLUB was founded in 1884 as 'Leicester Fosse', named after the Fosse Road, moving to Filbert Street in 1891. Known as The Foxes, their most famous former player is GARY LINEKER, now the BBC football anchorman and pundit. He was born in the city in 1960 and went to school there. His father was a greengrocer in Leicester's famous market. Lineker was made a freeman of the city in 1995 and is sometimes called 'Leicester's favourite son'. He has appeared in several TV commercials for Walkers, the snack foods company based in Leicester, and for a time in the 1990s they apparently gave their salt and vinegar crisps the name 'Salt-n-Lineker'!

THE LEICESTER TIGERS are a leading club in English ruby and one of the most successful clubs in the world. Founded in 1880 at a meeting in the George Hotel Leicester, they were called The Tigers as early as five years later. The name may have been connected with their brown and yellow kit at the time or linked to a local regiment with that nickname who served in India.

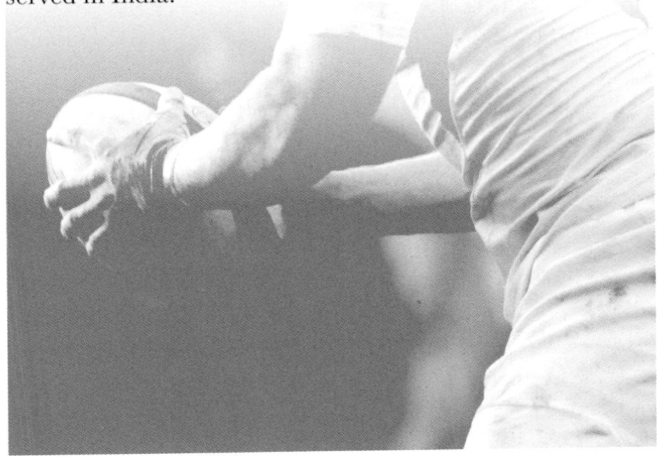

Some Village Voices from Leicestershire

Here is a selection of comments by some long-term residents of Leicestershire villages. They were interviewed in 2011 and 2012 for the *Village Voices* project referred to in the Introduction.

A resident of Thringstone, aged 75, recalls one of the sounds she used to associate with the village when she was growing up there:

> *… in the village at that time we'd only got … I think I'm right in saying … five gas lamps … and the hissin' of them if … we didn't go out much at night but if we did … it were nice to get from one hissin' bit to the other…*

A resident of Frisby-on-the-Wreake, aged 77, reflects on changes he has noticed in village community life:

> *… things take place in the village but some people … you never see them at anything … they just sleep here … and I think this is typical of a lot of villages these days … no matter … I mean you've got the chapel, the church, the pub, village hall … and you'll never see them at any of them … which is I think it's a shame … because you think … ask yourself well why do you come and live in the village?*

A resident of Coleorton, aged 60, recalls his schooldays in the village:

> *...we learnt most of the favourite hymns by heart and we also had singing of what I can best describe as country songs ... and we also did country dancing [...] I also recall that during the summer months we 'ad a good many nature walks with Mr Smith ... I didn't realise it at the time but the area was rich in wildlife ... we used to go round the fishpond and walk towards Farmtown and a good many species of plants and animals were pointed out to us...*

A retired farmer from Lubenham talks about the accents of children in the village today:

> *I think there's a slight difference to when we were younger because I think they're influenced by so many things now ... I think a lot of them are influenced by people who've moved into the village because a lot of families ... the children are ... they're the children of people who've moved into the village not actually long-term residents' children so they're bringing that slight influence of their parents with them and so there is a slight change ... but some that've grown up in the village from really young babies... they sort of sound really local don't they so I think there still is a slight village accent.*

As comments by older villagers show, there is an awareness that small communities in the county are undergoing considerable social change, some adapting more easily than others. This can be unsettling and makes people fear that, just as their green spaces have been eroded, so the local dialect is being 'diluted' and may disappear altogether.

However, a living language always changes and its dialects do the same, and this is not in itself a sign of decline, as we see from developments through the history of English. In highly populated areas like the East Midlands, many young people, including those who speak other languages too of course, are still growing up acquiring the modern dialect of this county, shaping it and making it their own, whether in the city, the market towns or villages. So they, too, are very likely to say in the future that people from other places in Britain can tell they come from Leicestershire.

Websites of Leicestershire and/or dialect interest

www.myleicestershire.org.uk

www.leicestershirevillages.com

www.le.ac.uk/emoha

www.knittingtogether.org.uk

www.sounds.bl.uk/Accents-and-dialects

Acknowledgements

I'd like to thank the Heritage Wardens of Leicestershire who acted as volunteer fieldworkers for the 'Village Voices: heritage in accents and dialect project in 2011 and 2012'. My thanks also go to Liz Blood of Leicestershire County Council's heritage services and to Colin Hyde, Director of the East Midlands Oral History Archive, for their help and support.

Select Bibliography

ELVERSTONE, ROBERT. 2014. *Absent through Want of Boots: Diary of a Victorian School in Leicestershire.* Stroud: The History Press.

EVANS, SEBASTIAN (ed.). 1881. *Leicestershire Words, Phrases and Proverbs* [collected by Arthur Benoni Evans]. Published for the English Dialect Society. London: Trubner & Co.

HICKMAN, TREVOR. 2003. *The Best of Leicestershire.* Stroud: Sutton Publishing Limited.

HOLDEN, LEN AND CHAMBERS, LINDA. 2008. *Market Harborough: Landscapes and Legends.* Donaghadee, N. Ireland: Cottage Publications.

MACAULAY, A. [Rev.] 1791.*The History and Antiquities of Claybrook*. Printed by J. Nichols.

PALMER, ROY. 1985. *The Folklore of Leicestershire and Rutland.* Wymondham: Sycamore Press.

ROBINSON, JONATHAN. 2015. *Evolving English WordBank.* Sheffield: Bradwell Books.

STEVENSON, JOAN. 1995. *Leicester through the Ages.* Newtown Linford: Kairos Press.

TAYLOR, MICHAEL AND WILSON, GEORGE. 1997. *The Quality of Leicester.* Revised second edition. Leicester: Leicester City Council.

WOOD, MICHAEL. 2010. *The Story of England.* London: Viking.